Original title:
How to Live Without Knowing Why

Copyright © 2025 Creative Arts Management OÜ
All rights reserved.

Author: Samuel Kensington
ISBN HARDBACK: 978-1-80566-033-0
ISBN PAPERBACK: 978-1-80566-328-7

The River of Uncertainty

I paddled my boat with a bristle of doubt,
My oars were just sticks, but they rocked me about.
The current was wild, but I laughed as I swayed,
Splashing my worries like they were just lemonade.

A fish offered wisdom, with scales shining bright,
"Chill out," it winked, "you'll be fine quite tonight!"
The river asked questions, I danced down the bend,
Sing me your answer, or better yet, just pretend!

Echoes of a Nameless Journey

I took a wrong turn on a road paved with glee,
Signed posts were confused, just like me.
But laughter was loud in the twilight's embrace,
And I stuffed all my cares in a suitcase of grace.

A rooster asked questions, the sun cracked a joke,
"Is this heaven or just the wildest folk?"
I shrugged, raised a toast with a banana in hand,
"Just wing it, my friend, it's a curious land!"

Tapestries of the Unbeheld

I stitched up my dreams with a needle of mirth,
Fabricated whims became silly rebirth.
With threads of confusion, I wove quite a tale,
A scarf for my thoughts on a shimmering trail.

The rabbits wore hats made of yesterday's news,
Dancing in circles, they refused to snooze.
Their laughter was echoing through clouds of delight,
Celebrating the riddle that makes wrong feel right.

Resonance of an Untold Story

In the library of chaos, I found a lost book,
Its pages were blank—now that's quite a hook!
I read it aloud to a peanut-shaped friend,
He chuckled and clapped, said, "Let's pretend!"

Every chapter was blank, but we filled it with cheer,
Monkeys on bicycles zoomed in and near.
With giggles and bubbles, we danced through the plot,
Creating a saga that's tasty and hot!

Dreams Unbound by Reason

In a land where socks sing glee,
Giraffes wear hats and dance with me.
We chase the clouds, we race the rain,
With jellybeans instead of pain.

Banana peels provide the groove,
As kangaroos in crocs approve.
Logic takes a nap, it snores,
While we explore through candy doors.

Floating on the Edge of Sense

Kites made of pancakes fly along,
A party with spoons singing a song.
We juggle dreams, and giggle in jest,
As penguins play chess, you know the best.

Mice wear ties, the cats wear shoes,
Confetti falls as we sip on blues.
Upside down, the world feels right,
In a circus where logic takes flight.

Moments Did Not Ask

Tick-tock went the clock with flair,
It tickled time, but who would care?
We shuffle feet on spaghetti strands,
As fish give speeches on empty lands.

Whispers of ice cream tease the night,
As rollie pollies join the fight.
"Why not?" we say with a happy grin,
As unicorns do the twist and spin.

Chasing Shadows of Meaning

Waffles walk in fancy shoes,
Chasing shadows of reds and blues.
Socks converse in witty rhymes,
As we jump through interpreting climes.

Fish in top hats discuss the sky,
While pop tarts bloom and waltz nearby.
"What's it all for?" we wink and cheer,
The answer's as clear as swimming with beer.

Grounded in Uncertainty

Woke up this morning, quite unsure,
What's for breakfast? Maybe a cure?
Pancakes or waffles? Choices galore,
But my fridge says 'Maybe, check back for more.'

Sock on my foot, not a matching pair,
Who needs convention? I don't really care.
Chasing the cat with my coffee in hand,
What if the milk wanders off to a land?

Treading Water in a Sea of Doubt

Jump in the pool, but where's the deep end?
Is it safe? Perhaps I should just pretend.
Swim with the floaties, it's quite the show,
Rubber ducks giggle, they know how to flow.

Questions like soap bubbles drift up to the sky,
Pop one, and giggles come tumbling by.
What's after 'why'? I'm starting to fear,
The answer's just waiting with snacks and a beer.

Stars that Shine in Obscurity

Stars twinkle bright in a cloudy night dome,
Wish upon one, then grab your ice cream cone.
Who knows their stories? Just float there and smile,
Maybe they're just trying to make us their style.

Wish I were a comet, with tails made of pie,
Whipping past raccoons who look up and sigh.
Each star's a puzzle, no need to be wise,
Lay back, keep munching, let mysteries rise.

The Breath Between Purpose

In the pause of the day, a hiccup or two,
Questions hang in the air, like socks on the loo.
Why does the toast always land butter-side down?
Maybe it's laughter that spins us around.

Dancing in circles, we chase our own feet,
Life's an odd rhythm, a whimsical beat.
In moments of silence, a giggle resides,
Between every heartbeat, where nonsense abides.

A Song Without Lyrics

In the park, a dog does prance,
Chasing squirrels, lost in dance.
Who needs a plan, a script, a rhyme?
Life's best moments run out of time.

With a hat too large, I stroll the street,
Umbrella in hand, but no rain to greet.
Each day's a show, we laugh, we jive,
Like a joke with no punchline, just to survive.

On the couch, two cats collide,
One's in control, the other, a ride.
Pillows become castles, dreams without maps,
While naps are the mission, no need for mishaps.

So let's toast to the silly, the absurdly bright,
Living it up, with all our might.
With no grand reason, we make our way,
In this madcap world, we're here to play.

The Stillness of Lively Hearts

A goldfish swims round in a bowl,
Thinking of fishy dreams, oh so droll.
It knows not why it swims in circles,
Yet finds joy in the ripples and sparkles.

In a café, a man sips tea,
Counting the crumbs, what can they be?
They giggle 'bout cookies, he can't decide,
Without a reason, he melts with pride.

A child in the sandbox, molding her dream,
Building a kingdom without a theme.
While birds overhead argue their song,
Life is a ditty, and nothing feels wrong.

So here we tumble, laugh and cheer,
With whimsy and wonder, forgetting the fear.
For life is a whimsy, a curious art,
In the stillness of lively, unknowing hearts.

The Rhythm of Wandering Souls

In a world where answers hide,
We dance with questions, side by side.
Like socks that vanish in the wash,
Our logic trips, a silly bosh.

With maps of nonsense in our hands,
We stroll through life, making grand stands.
Chasing rainbows, sipping gloom,
We find delight in a cluttered room.

Beyond the Grasp of Certainty

We ponder over cups of tea,
Do fish ever wish to fly free?
In riddles wrapped in bubble wrap,
We laugh and lose our silly map.

Seeking truth in jello molds,
Life's mystery like tales untold.
We stumble forth, a joyous parade,
Unraveling knots that never were made.

Reflections on the Edge of Knowing

With mirrors cracked and views askew,
We joke about what we never knew.
A turtle runs, a snail takes flight,
In the circus of our mind, it's quite a sight.

Peeking through our kaleidoscope,
We wear confusion like a cape of hope.
Every misstep a dance routine,
Life's quirks are quirky and quite routine.

Unwritten Tales of the Heart

Oh, the tales that we all hoard,
Pineapple pizza? A strange reward.
With hearts like jellybeans in a jar,
We jest of journeys to lands afar.

In scribbled notes and goofy dreams,
We plot our fates in silly schemes.
With laughter echoing through the night,
We celebrate the wrongs that feel so right.

Sailing on Questions

On a boat made of hope, we drift and we sway,
With no compass in hand, we laugh all the way.
Each wave holds a riddle, a joke in disguise,
We navigate nonsense with wide-open eyes.

A seagull named Larry shouts answers quite loud,
But his wisdom is buried in hot dog and crowd.
We fish for the meaning of life on a line,
But our catch is just giggles and sandwich divine.

The Weight of Unsung Songs

A melody lives in the space of the mind,
But who wrote the lyrics? We're completely blind!
With a ukulele made from a shoelace and glue,
We strum out a tune to the sky that's so blue.

The chorus is silly, the verses absurd,
Yet we belt out our thoughts, undeterred, undeterred!
With each off-key note, we dance in delight,
For who needs the meaning when laughter takes flight?

Lanterns in the Mist

In a fog where we wander, we light up the way,
With lanterns of giggles that brighten the gray.
Each flicker a question, each shadow a smile,
We roam through the unknown, embracing the style.

The monsters are friendly, they tap dance around,
With socks on their feet, they don't make a sound.
In this whimsical maze, we twirl and we spin,
Ignoring the why while we bask in our grin.

Fragmented Paths and Broken Dreams

On a trail made of donuts, we stumble and slip,
With each sugary step, we take another trip.
The map is a doodle, the signs make no sense,
Yet we skip along boldly, our laughter intense.

Our dreams are like puzzles, all mixed in a box,
With pieces of jellybeans and mismatched socks.
But each colorful fragment is bright as a flare,
As we dance through the chaos without a care!

Emptiness Wearing a Smile

A jester's cap upon my head,
I skip through life, my thoughts misled.
With laughter loud, I hide the void,
In playful pranks, my fears destroyed.

Each morning greets a fresh delight,
Like juggling balls in fading light.
I twirl and spin, the world my stage,
With silly faces, I turn the page.

Yet deep within, a puzzle waits,
A riddle locked behind the gates.
But who has time for worry's frown?
I'll paint my face and clowns the town.

So come and join this merry chase,
With every laugh, I'll find my place.
In empty rooms where echoes cheer,
I'll wear my smile, embrace the queer.

Corners of Forgotten Whispers

In dusty nooks where shadows creep,
I brush aside the thoughts so deep.
With giggles tucked in secrets tight,
I dance with echoes late at night.

The whispers tease, they speak in jest,
Of things unreal, no time for rest.
With humor bright, I stride along,
To rewrite tales, where I belong.

The wisdom of a socked-up sock,
Is clearer than a ticking clock.
I chase the breeze, I chase the sound,
Amongst the whispers, laughter's found.

So let us twirl in circles wide,
With every spin, we'll cast aside.
The corners hold their secrets tight,
But in our laughter, all's alright.

Dances with Doubt

With two left feet, I take the floor,
In clumsy moves, I seek for more.
A sloppy waltz, a tango missed,
I laugh and twirl, can't resist.

Doubt sends signals, a baffled mime,
But who needs rhythm? I've got time.
I shuffle sideways, take a leap,
In this uncertainty, joy runs deep.

A pirouette in fuzzy socks,
I trip on thoughts, then write my knocks.
With every stumble, I find my beat,
As life's a dance, and oh, so sweet.

So come and laugh at all the slips,
Let's twirl our doubts with silly flips.
With every misstep, we'll come alive,
In this merry chaos, we will thrive!

The Unwritten Chapters

An open book with pages bare,
I pen my thoughts with utmost care.
The ink is blue, the humor bright,
In sketches bold, I take to flight.

I scribble tales of quirky fame,
Of talking dogs and men named Tame.
With wild adventures, plots awry,
I chase the clouds across the sky.

Each chapter hints at laughter's call,
With silly plots, I risk it all.
For life's a script that's never done,
In joyful chaos, we all run.

So grab your pens and join the fun,
In unwritten tales where we outrun.
With every giggle, every cheer,
We write our lives, no hint of fear.

Puzzles with Missing Pieces

Life's a jigsaw, pieces laid,
Some fit well, others just delayed.
Noses on dogs, not in the frame,
We laugh at it all, that's part of the game.

Clue books lost in the trash, they say,
We search for answers, come what may.
But if every piece just fits so tight,
What fun would it be, to live with fright?

A Heart that Beats in Mystery

A tick-tock heart, with no advice,
Flutters for pizza, no need for rice.
It sings a tune, quite off the beat,
Dances on toes, spaghetti's treat.

What makes it thump, we cannot know,
Is it love or just a new shoe glow?
With twists and turns, my heart's a show,
A circus act, where feelings grow.

Fragments of Clarity in Confusion

In a foggy maze, direction's a game,
I found my way, through a cat's meow fame.
Maps are for wizards, I'll take the strange,
With fuzzy logic, let's exchange.

Lemonade thoughts on a cloudy day,
Sipped with a laugh, in a fizzy sway.
When clarity's fleeting and confusion's spacious,
I cling to my puns, they're simply gracious.

Notes from an Unanswered Song

A melody hums, with no end in sight,
Missing the words that feel just right.
I tap my toes to the offbeat sound,
With laughter and joy is where I'm found.

Each note a tickle, a tease of delight,
A dance with shadows in the soft moonlight.
Though answers elude, I'm all in the zone,
With giggles and grins, I'm never alone.

Roads Unraveled by Mystery

I wandered down a crooked street,
With twists and turns, no end in sight.
I grinned at every sign I met,
"Turn left at confusion!" what a fright.

A bird just laughed, its feathers bright,
"Why question why? Just take a stroll."
I danced along without a care,
Who knew that joy could be so whole?

Each corner held a surprise or two,
A juggler dropped his hat and sighed.
I laughed and joined the silly crew,
"Embrace the chaos!" was my guide.

So if you trip, just take a bow,
The world's a stage without a script.
With every fall, the laughter grows,
A mystery box that can't be zipped.

The Freedom of Not Knowing

Why ask the stars for hints so grand,
When rolling dice can be such fun?
I'll spin a tale with no set plan,
Life's a game that can't be won.

I wear my shorts the wrong way round,
Why match my socks? It's quite absurd.
Each clueless move is joy unbound,
In chaos, I'm the wisest bird.

No need for maps or set destinations,
I'll dance along the random path.
With every trip, pure exhilaration,
I'll skip through life, embracing math.

So here's to us, the lost but free,
No answers needed, just take a leap.
With chuckles bright and hearts so light,
Embrace the weird, let laughter seep.

Inscribing Our Lives in the Dark

In shadowed corners where we stay,
I scribble dreams with candlelight.
Who needs a guide when we can play,
With words that dance beyond the night?

A pirate's hat, a wizard's cloak,
I'm dressed to thrill in my own tale.
Each scribbled line's a gentle joke,
Exploring paths where senses fail.

The darkness hums a playful tune,
A riddle wrapped in cotton fluff.
With every quirk, I find my boon,
No need for truth, that's just too tough.

So here I pen my goofy plight,
A world that giggles while I write.
In shadows deep, creativity burns,
With every squiggle, the heart upturns.

Beneath the Veil of Complacency

In chairs that squeak, we lounge around,
Planned routines hold us like a net.
But what if we just flipped it down,
And lost the plot without a fret?

The toaster dances with delight,
Each morning brings a fresh surprise.
I skipped my coffee, felt alright,
Who knew the world had such wild cries?

With every shrug, we toss the script,
Let lists go flying in the air.
A life unscripted turns the tide,
Where joy blooms bright and without care.

So let the dishes pile and stack,
We'll toast to chaos, a crazy feast.
Embrace the fun, don't hold it back,
In comfy bliss, we're truly released.

Trusting the Uncharted

In a world where ducks wear hats,
I skip stones while chasing chats.
Sometimes the road is full of fog,
But I dance with a perplexed dog.

Maps are just suggestions, you see,
I follow my nose, not a decree.
The sun might shine or rain might pour,
Still, I'll sing like a weathered lore.

With socks that don't quite match their pair,
I wade through life without a care.
If the cheese is blue, that's just fine,
I'll say it's aged like fine wine.

So let's toast to the silly unknown,
Where questions sprout but answers have flown.
We'll juggle our whims, let fate decide,
In wobbly boats, we'll take the tide.

The Canvas of Unknowing

Brush in hand, I paint the air,
My canvas? A chair that's bare.
Swirls of laughter, streaks of doubt,
Each stroke beckons a merry pout.

Pasting dreams of polka dots,
While the cat dangles from the pots.
Colors clash, yet they harmonize,
An art show for the unwise.

Who needs a plan, or brush with might?
I splatter joy, then take a flight.
With squirrels as critics, I stand tall,
My masterpiece? A silly sprawl.

So grab a paint can, laugh and play,
The art of living's a holiday.
In the mix of jest and pure delight,
We'll find our spark in every blight.

Untangled Threads of Fate

A spider spins without a care,
While I trip on my laces bare.
The threads of fate are quite the mess,
Yet, I wear socks that say 'bless!'

Twists and turns in every dance,
Learning life just takes a chance.
With spaghetti arms, I'll twirl about,
As confused as a lost trout.

I'll stitch my dreams with silly fears,
And drown them in jubilant cheers.
Each knot tied with a laugh or two,
What could be worse than not having glue?

So here's to tangles, bold and bright,
Where every wrong is a sheer delight.
Together we'll weave a zany song,
At the end of the day, we all belong.

Surrendering to the Present

A slice of pie beneath a tree,
I ponder why that squirrel's free.
With a giggle, I take a bite,
And let the world spin with delight.

Birds chirp like they've won a prize,
Enquanto I watch clouds chase the skies.
If time decides to dance away,
I'll shimmy right into the fray.

Every now and then life's a jest,
The best moments? They won't rest.
With sprinkles on top of this cake called time,
I'll ride the rhythms, feel the rhyme.

So let's celebrate the goofy grace,
Each tick is a chance, a zany space.
Embrace the now, in all its fettle,
Life's a wild song, let's dance and settle!

Steps without a Compass

I wander through the tangled trees,
With socks that clash and knees that please.
I trip on roots, I laugh and roll,
Seeking the point, but lose the goal.

Each turn I take leads to a wall,
A puzzled look, my friends all call.
I smile wide, I giggle loud,
Finding joy in being unbowed.

The map's a mess, it's skating rinks,
With penguins as my guiding links.
I dance with glee down every street,
And count the flowers at my feet.

No north, no south, just laughs galore,
In this wild quest, who needs more?
With every step in total dread,
I stumble forth, with joy ahead.

Chasing the Invisible

I'm sprinting fast, but hit a brick,
Chasing shadows is my new trick.
The grasshoppers laugh, and I join in,
As the world spins round, a dizzying spin.

Invisible things, oh what a chase,
I'll catch that glare, I'm setting the pace.
With paper wings, I soar too high,
A tumble here, a giggle, and sigh.

A bubble pops, mystery solved,
Was I even here? Problem unresolved!
I sip on air, it has no taste,
Chasing the void, in laughter I'm based.

Come join this dance where nothing is real,
We'll spin and twirl with gleeful zeal.
In this mad chase, we'll find a spark,
The invisible things light up the dark.

The Quest for Meaningless Joy

On a quest for laughter, I ride a duck,
In oversized shoes, just my luck!
Silly songs drive the dull away,
As I prance along all night and day.

A treasure map with no 'X' mark,
Leads me to giggles in the park.
Who needs a point? I've got my crew,
With nonsense games and sticky goo.

Chasing bubbles the size of my head,
Pop, pop, pop, on this journey I tread.
The clock strikes five, but who's keeping time?
In search of joy, we make our rhyme.

We plant our flags on a pile of fun,
No lessons learned, but oh, what a run!
In lifelong laughter, we all rejoice,
On the quest for joy, find your own voice.

A Map of Unmapped Roads

I open a map, upside down—
Lost in the lines, away from town.
With doodles of cows and a dragon's tail,
My navigator's a jingling snail.

Each road I take twists up and down,
With a tumble and fall, I wear a crown.
The dirt path leads to a frosty pie,
I nibble away while wondering why.

The compass spins, it's on a break,
I point to the sun, but it gives a shake.
With every wrong turn, a giggling spree,
As the universe chuckles, just me and me.

A map of dreams in color and cheer,
I'll wander long and hold laughter near.
As I meander down these hidden ways,
Life's a joke, let's spend our days!

Lighthouses in the Dark

In a foggy haze, we dance with glee,
Chasing shadows, just you and me.
Navigating life like a ship gone astray,
With laughter as our guide, we'll find our way.

We stumble on rocks, but who really cares?
With clumsy grace, we burst into flares.
Lighthouses wink with a playful spark,
Illuminating smiles, igniting the dark.

The map is blank, oh what a treat!
Wandering paths on mismatched feet.
Each step a joke, a giggle, a sigh,
Who needs a reason when you can fly high?

So here we are, lost but not blue,
An adventure awaits, we'll see it through.
With quirks and laughs, the moments align,
Lighthouses flicker, saying, "It's fine!"

Stillness in the Storm

Raindrops fall like confetti balloons,
While we sip tea in our paper-thin rooms.
The world is a whirl, but we find our calm,
Strumming sweet chords, like a soothing balm.

Thunder claps with a comic twist,
We'll dance to the rhythm, we simply insist.
Not even the winds can mess with our cheer,
Bouncing in puddles, we've nothing to fear.

We wear clouds as our stylish hats,
A fashion statement, not for the flats.
Stillness found in chaos around,
In storms, our laughter is the loudest sound.

So when the sky tosses tempests our way,
We giggle and wiggle, come what may.
With joy in our hearts and quirks galore,
We'll weather the storms, then ask for more!

Sweetness in the Absence

Empty chairs with crumbs of delight,
Memories linger like stars at night.
Missing the cake but loving the grin,
In absence we find the sweetness within.

A joke that's told on a silent street,
Echoes of laughter that sway to the beat.
Ghosts of good times in the air we share,
In the emptiness blooms a love that's rare.

Banana peels slip; we giggle a ton,
In the missing pieces, we've already won.
For what we don't have, we still celebrate,
With pie charts of joy, we navigate fate.

Sweetness found in the gaps we create,
In absence, our hearts find a playful state.
So here's to the spaces where laughter builds,
In the quiet alone, our spirit fulfilled.

Chronicles of the Inexplicit

Once upon a time, or maybe not,
A tale of mishaps, connections forgot.
Wibbly-wobbly, the plot makes no sense,
But who needs logic when fun is immense?

A cat wore a hat, while ducks took a stroll,
Dancing in circles, that's how they roll.
Every misstep is a chapter we heed,
In chronicles full of whimsical need.

Monkeys in suits discuss the weather,
While penguins juggle with no end tethered.
Inexplicit dreams that tickle the mind,
With each twist and turn, new laughs we find.

So gather your friends, let's start this tale,
Of silly antics that'll never pale.
In the book of goofs, we all play a part,
Chronicles formed from the joy of the heart.

Silent Threads of Existence

In a world of tangled strings,
We dance like puppets on a whim,
Joking with the moonlit kings,
While time slips through, ever dim.

Laughter bubbles in the air,
As squirrels plot their great escape,
Quirky tales beyond compare,
What's the point? We'll just reshape.

Life's a puzzle, missing pieces,
Yet still we smile with glee,
In confusion, joy increases,
Here we are, just being free.

With every step, a funny fate,
Like cats that think they own the world,
Stumbling on, it's never late,
In silly dreams our flags unfurled.

The Question Mark of Tomorrow

A feather floats upon the breeze,
Will it land? Who really knows!
Each uncertain twist aims to tease,
Socks and sandals—the latest shows!

Grumpy clouds can roll and frown,
But we just dance in puddles wide,
Why not smile, flip upside down?
Mirth is the universe's guide.

Wanderlust without a plan,
Like penguins in a pizza store,
Life's more fun without a scan,
Just roll the dice and watch it soar!

Tomorrow? Oh, it's just a blur,
Wrapped in mystery and delight,
We chase the fun, no time to stir,
Laughing till the stars ignite.

Shadows in the Unseen Light

Underneath the bright facade,
We wander down the paths unknown,
Curious, we jest and prod,
With shadows where the laughter's grown.

The sun might hide behind a wall,
Yet we can find our way with prance,
In every stumble, every fall,
We pirouette in this wild dance!

Pigeons plot their little schemes,
While we sip coffee, lost in thought,
Life's a sitcom, bursting seams,
With punchlines that can't be bought.

Oh, the joy in shadows played,
Twinkling stars in every laugh,
No need for maps, we're unafraid,
With humor as our quirky craft.

Unwritten Paths of a Wandering Soul

A wandering soul with paper shoes,
Dances like a leaf on high,
Choosing whims like a picky muse,
Along the trails where questions lie.

Maps are for the dull and meek,
As we paint the sky in vivid hues,
Turning bumps into chic mystique,
Filling our pockets with silly dues.

Answering a riddle or two,
Tickling fate with a cheerful sprawl,
The stars provide a jig or cue,
As laughter echoes through the hall.

With every heartbeat, let's explore,
To leap where whimsy takes its flight,
In this grand game, we'll never bore,
In blissful chats with day and night.

The Freedom of Not Knowing

In a world of tasty snacks,
I dance without a clue,
Like a cat on roller skates,
Just hoping not to spew.

With each misstep I take,
I chuckle and I grin,
Life's a wild adventure,
Let the chaos begin!

Maps are just suggestions,
I follow where I stray,
Each fork is a new path,
In my goofball ballet.

So raise a glass of jelly,
To moments that go fast,
For in the joy of wiggles,
We find the best laughs last.

A Journey without a Map

I set out on my journey,
A compass spinning wild,
Following the fluffiest clouds,
Like a curious child.

With snacks stuffed in my pockets,
And a bird that sings off-key,
I wander through the garden,
In search of mystery.

The road may twist and tangle,
But I just twirl and sway,
In every blunder, giggles,
Keep boredom far away.

Each step is filled with laughter,
In the sunshine's friendly glow,
With mismatched socks and sandals,
Letting winds of whimsy blow.

The Beauty of Fleeting Moments

Like bubbles in champagne,
They shimmer and they grace,
Each moment is a giggle,
A quick and silly face.

I chase the fleeting shadows,
With giggles on my trail,
In life's grand circus, darling,
I'm the clown without a veil.

Moments zip like fireflies,
They wink and then they're gone,
I catch them in my laughter,
Until the break of dawn.

So let's dance in the darkness,
And swim in waves of light,
Each fleeting, funny moment,
Fills our hearts with delight.

When Silence Speaks Louder

In a room where laughter shrinks,
And the quiet takes a seat,
The silence spills like jelly,
A funny little treat.

With my thoughts running loops,
Like a hamster on a wheel,
I ponder on the unspoken,
In a comedy of zeal.

The pauses stretch like taffy,
With giggles in between,
Life's a mime in motions,
So silly and so keen.

And when the stillness lingers,
Like an awkward dance encore,
We find that joy's contagious,
In the quiet, hear the roar!

The Beauty of not Understanding

Woke up in a messy room,
Socks on my ears, it's a comical tune.
Coffee spills and breakfast burns,
Yet joy in chaos, my heart still yearns.

A dance with confusion, a twirl and a spin,
Who needs a map when you've got the grin?
Lost in a world where nonsense is gold,
Each laugh a treasure, more precious than bold.

Gazes into the Abyss

Staring deep into the empty cup,
Wondering which of the beans will erupt.
Is it coffee or dreams that keep me awake?
The abyss chuckles, for goodness' sake!

The void waves back, with a wink and a nod,
"Life's just a riddle, not an easy prod."
Tickling my brain with thoughts that will stray,
Who cares about reason? Just join in the play!

The Unseen Pathways

Walking on roads that lead to nowhere,
Each step I take, a whimsical dare.
Crickets recite their nightly tunes,
Under the glow of confused, happy moons.

Maps made of jellybeans and fluff,
Navigating laughter, is never enough!
Paths woven of giggles, tangled in fun,
Blindfolded discoveries, oh what a run!

Echoing Silence of the Mind

In the silence, my thoughts take flight,
Chasing the shadows, a playful sight.
Whispers of nonsense dance in the air,
While logic rolls over, not knowing to care.

Silly ideas bounce, like rubber balls,
Swirling around these echoing halls.
Why think too deeply when laughter's the key?
Nonsensical joy, come play with me!

Footprints on Untrodden Soil

In a field where no one goes,
I dance like a chicken, striking a pose.
My footprints trace a silly line,
While squirrels look on, sipping their wine.

The sun sneezes bright, I trip and slide,
Laughing at life, my daily ride.
Ignoring the rules, I frolic and play,
Tomorrow feels lost, but hey, that's okay.

A snail joins in, with swagger so grand,
Dressed up in shells, like beads on a strand.
We waltz through the grass, my odd little crew,
Making up games, not a clue in the blue.

So here's to the paths we never will take,
With silly decisions, and big laughs to make.
Footprints so wild, they'll soon disappear,
But the fun is the goal -- the end's never near.

Kaleidoscope of Uncertain Colors

A bubblegum sky, with polka dot dreams,
Life spills in colors, bursting at seams.
Jellybean rain falls soft on my nose,
Where nonsense and whimsy collide in a pose.

I wear mismatched socks, a crown made of cheese,
Chasing butterflies, lost on the breeze.
My thoughts are a whirlpool of sweet taffy twists,
As I giggle aloud at the world that exists.

I ponder the stars, quite baffled yet spry,
Why do they twinkle? I can only sigh.
With rainbows and sparkles that dance in my head,
I'll sail through this puzzle, my own path instead.

Each day's a mosaic, all jumbled and bright,
In a kaleidoscope world, everything feels right.
So join in my chaos, let laughter be bold,
And paint all your worries in colors untold.

Holding onto the Inexplicable

A cat wearing socks, sipping on tea,
Is it normal? Does it bother thee?
I clutch at the oddities, near and far,
As I chat with my goldfish, beneath a star.

The moon winks at me, with secrets galore,
Whispers of nonsense, can't take it much more.
I juggle my thoughts like apples in air,
While painting the silence with glitter and flair.

I find all my puzzles in cupboards of spice,
Where cinnamon speaks and pepper is nice.
Each moment's a riddle, unpredictable fun,
As I skip through the chaos, under the sun.

So here I am, hugging the strange and bizarre,
Finding comfort in quirks, near and far.
In this carnival world, where logic can sway,
I'll hold onto riddles, come what may.

Journeying into the Abyss

With a sandwich in hand, I plunge into night,
Exploring the shadows, my trembling delight.
Is it dark? Is it deep? Oh, what a surprise,
As I trip on my shoelaces and argue with flies.

The abyss calls my name, a pit made of cheer,
Where laughter's the echo I'm longing to hear.
I find a lost sock and a tune from the past,
In a world full of giggles, I'll make it my cast.

On this journey of whimsy, I trip and I spin,
Through the mazes of nonsense, where do I begin?
Maybe the void leads to treasure unknown,
Like chocolate-flavored clouds or a mean old gnome.

So let's venture together, a plunge hand in hand,
Into the abyss where it's all rather grand.
With giggles and mischief, we'll rejoin the light,
Without knowing the reason – it just feels so right.

Whispers in the Void

In a room full of shoes, no one knows,
Why I only wear two, but goodness, it shows.
Dancing with shadows, they wiggle and sway,
I laugh at their silliness, come what may.

Why do squirrels chatter above in the trees?
I ask them for wisdom, they just say, "Cheese!"
Life's riddles wrapped tight in a bright yellow bow,
With answers elusive, like a runaway crow.

Jellybeans speak in riddles at night,
They argue with socks, it gives me a fright!
Though questions are many, my answers are few,
The void whispers softly, and giggles ensue.

The moon winks at me, full of moonlit delight,
As stars take their shots, a cosmic goodnight.
So I'll frolic in laughter, and dance through the haze,
Life's a nonsensical puzzle, in so many ways.

Navigating the Unknown

A rubber chicken serves as my guide,
Through mazes of nonsense, my trusted side.
With compasses spinning and maps upside down,
I laugh at the frowns of the lost and the found.

Banana peels trail where the answers might be,
But I slip on the questions, oh woe is me!
The mystery grows like a cat's crazy hair,
I pet the absurd while the sane just stare.

With googly eyes, I seek out the truth,
But the truth plays tag, a mischievous sleuth.
I'm lost in the puzzle of pie and of cake,
Laughing at life's gaffes for fun's sacred sake.

So I waltz with confusion and skip with the fun,
Embracing the chaos, I'm never done!
With rubber ducks quacking, I sail on the breeze,
As laughter erupts from the depths of the trees.

Embrace of the Unsung

I wear mismatched socks for a reason unclear,
Each one whispers secrets I hold dear.
In a world of the blandness, I crave a good jest,
With laughter my armor, I'm truly blessed.

The toaster burnt bread with a giggling sigh,
As if it's a joke that we both can't deny.
I hum to the rhythm of socks in the wash,
Life's unsung melodies, all silly and posh.

A jester appears, clad in colorful hues,
With a dance and a jig that steals my blues.
The unspoken tales of the odd and the weird,
Bring smiles and mischief; my heart is endeared.

So I cuddle the absurd in a warm, silly hug,
As whimsy and wonder flow like a drug.
In the embrace of the unsung, I find my delight,
With laughter the compass that guides me at night.

Life's Fragile Enigma

Like a bubble that floats on a whispering breeze,
Life's fragile enigma teases with ease.
I dance with the whimsy of fate's silly games,
While juggling my dreams with some wild, wacky claims.

A cat on a skateboard, a dog in a hat,
Are signs from the universe, imagine that!
Each flicker of laughter, a spark on my face,
In the circus of life, I find my place.

Why do we worry 'bout things that won't stick?
Like sticky tape flies in a slapstick flick.
The mysteries linger, like crumbs on my shirt,
Yet joy's the adventure, for what it is worth.

So I twirl through the questions, surreal and absurd,
With the wisdom of soup cans, laughing unheard.
In the fragile enigma where giggles abound,
I celebrate folly, where joy can be found.

Searching for Meaning in the Faintest Stars

I looked up high, the sky's a mess,
Chasing thoughts in cosmic dress.
With a telescope made from tin foil,
Hoping wisdom won't recoil.

They say the stars have wisdom bright,
Yet they twinkle, just out of sight.
I wondered if I'm born to seek,
Or just a cosmic, clueless freak.

In endless void, I sip my tea,
Searching meaning, but where's the key?
A shooting star whizzes right by,
Was that a sign, or just a fly?

So I dance under the twinkle glow,
Embrace the chaos, let it flow.
Laughing loudly at the great unknown,
For in confusion, I've found my home.

Traces of What Might Have Been

Once I dreamed of grand success,
Now I'm here in comfy dress.
Thought I'd chase what I could be,
But I tripped on a peanut, oh me!

I pondered paths I didn't take,
Danced with shadows, brewed some cake.
Each bite sang of missed delights,
At least my taste buds are all right!

I scribble plans on napkin sheets,
While munching down on leftovers' sweets.
In life's great game, I've lost a round,
But who knew joy could be profound?

So I toast to what I never tried,
With a steaming mug, and arms spread wide.
Every trace of missed chances reflects,
A life well spent, with no regrets!

The Ritual of Being Present

I meditate while eating my fries,
Crunching loudly, then close my eyes.
In bacon dreams, I find my grace,
Focused bliss on my greasy face.

I walk my dog, and he moves fast,
I wonder if he's pondering the past.
Is he thinking of chasing that cat?
Or just waiting for me to sit and chat?

The clock ticks slow on lazy days,
As I ponder all life's quirky ways.
Is the meaning deep or just a wink?
Maybe it's found in how we think?

So let's embrace this awkward dance,
Life's a circus; just take a chance.
Laughing loudly, with all your might,
Is the best way to feel alright!

In the Lap of Ambiguity

I float along on waves of doubt,
In a boat made from a pizza route.
With pepperoni sails set to go,
I'm not quite sure, but hey, it's a show!

I chat with clouds about their plight,
While they rain on my enthusiasm bright.
Are they crying, or just having fun?
I laugh as I dance in an umbrella run.

Ambiguous paths lead me around,
On trails where lost socks can be found.
Do I forge ahead or stall in play?
Maybe just wing it day by day?

So let's toast to the foggy paths,
Raise a glass to the cosmic laughs.
In confusion, I find my spree,
For life's greatest joy is just to be!

Embracing the Unknown's Embrace

In a world where wonders sway,
I don pajamas every day.
Chasing dreams, I trip and fall,
But laughter's still my favorite call.

Like socks that never match, it seems,
I wade through puddles of my dreams.
The sun may hide; the clouds may tease,
Yet I'll still dance with charming ease.

With spoons and forks I play a song,
No plan in mind; it can't be wrong.
The cosmic joke's a merry tune,
So I'll add my voice—let's sing, not croon.

So when the map's all blank and bare,
I'll make new paths, I won't despair.
Here's to the ride, the twists, the spins,
Life's a blast, let chaos begin!

Between Whispers and Echoes

Whispering winds, they tease my ear,
In the kitchen, I drop my beer.
A dance of thoughts, a jig of quirks,
In a world where chaos lurks.

Like a cat that thinks it's a dog,
Seeing clarity in the fog.
Questions tumble, no answer's found,
Yet joy abounds, it knows no bound.

Juggling life, with pies in the air,
I laugh at fate; it seems unfair.
But each wobbly step I take,
Leads to the cake I'm bound to make.

Between whispers and echoes, I glide,
With socks on my hands, I shall not hide.
For in the riddle, I find my fun,
Life's a race? Nah, I'd rather run!

Dancing Amidst the Void

In the void, where shadows play,
My dance is grand, though skies are gray.
With noodles as my flowing gown,
I twirl and whirl, I'm quite renowned!

Silent symphonies serenade,
Like clowns in make-up, unafraid.
With jellybeans to guide my way,
I hop through night, I leap through day.

I've lost my keys, but found a rhyme,
In every stumble, I'm rich with time.
So here's to the void, I lift my glass,
Cheers to the chaos, let moments pass!

With every twirl, unchained and free,
Life's a giggle, just wait and see.
So join my jig, come take a spin,
For dancing in voids is where we win!

The Art of Simply Being

In pjs soft, I start my day,
Without a clue of what to say.
I sip my coffee, spill it too,
Oh, what a life, so bright and blue!

With socks that slide on kitchen floors,
I glide through life, I open doors.
Laughter echoes without a cause,
In this sweet mess, I take a pause.

A friendly plant is all I need,
It talks to me in leaf and seed.
While questions fly like birds in flight,
I find my joy in silly light.

To simply be, I raise a cheer,
Without a map, I'm drawing near.
For in the art of just "to be,"
Life's canvas paints itself with glee!

Canvas of the Uncharted

Splashing paint without a clue,
Colors clash, laughter ensues,
Art is chaos, a wild spree,
Who knew it'd bring such glee?

Brush in hand, no map in sight,
Dancing swirls in the soft moonlight,
Mistakes become the new delight,
Is it wrong? Nah, that's quite right!

Each stroke a giggle, a twist of fate,
Scribbles that ponder, why hesitate?
On this canvas, joy only grows,
As the world outside simply dozes.

So let's embrace this wacky spree,
No grand meaning, just pure glee,
With colors bright and hearts alight,
In this uncharted, funny flight!

Finding Stillness in Chaos

In the whirlwind of life's loud song,
Why is the journey always so long?
We spin and twist, what a crazy dance,
Finding calm in life's mischance.

Giggles echo in the ruckus loud,
A quiet spot? Oh, good luck, crowd!
Yet in the mess, smiles bloom anew,
Who needs silence? Laughter will do!

Twirling minds like tops galore,
Seeking calm, but craving more,
A goofy grin on a daisy's face,
In utter chaos, we find our place.

So let's toast to the crazy times,
With clinking mugs and silly rhymes,
In the chaos, we are the jesters,
Finding stillness in our own festivals!

Threads of an Unraveled Tapestry

A knot in the yarn, what a delight,
Unraveling it makes for a funny sight,
The tapestry spills stories untold,
Laughing at threads that refuse to fold.

With a needle, I poke, and the cat goes wild,
Tangled laughter from this crafty child,
Patterns shift and colors play,
Who knew chaos could brighten the day?

A patchwork quilt of giggles and grins,
Each loop a memory, that's where it begins,
Forget the design, just throw in some fun,
In this funny mess, we have all won!

Let's stitch together this ludicrous tale,
With threads of joy that never grow stale,
An unraveled masterpiece, oh what a spree,
Life's artful mess is our recipe!

Breath of the Unseen

Invisible whispers tickle the air,
What does it mean? Do we dare?
Yet in the giggles, the nonsense peeks,
Breath of the unseen, it surely speaks.

Kites in the wind dance with glee,
Unseen forces pulling so free,
Up and about, we soar and glide,
Amid the laughter, we take our ride.

Each hiccup of joy, a bashful breeze,
In the unseen, let's do as we please,
Invisible cheerleading, cheering us on,
In this funny universe, we've all won!

So let us frolic, let us pretend,
No need to know, just follow the trend,
In laughter's breath, we find our key,
To living wild, where we're all free!

Musings of a Wandering Soul

A sock just vanished, who knows where?
Two left-footed dancers, pair without care.
Chasing shadows in a sunlit park,
Lost on a path that's just a spark.

Life's great mystery, a jester at play,
Why the chicken crossed? Who's to say?
I trip on laughter, tumble with glee,
Searching for answers hidden in tea.

Frogs in tuxedos sing sweet serenades,
While we ponder life, lost in charades.
Do lollipops dream of licorice nights?
Or do gummy bears plot in candy fights?

So here's to quests where logic gets bent,
Playing the fool, a delightful event.
With each silly step, I dance on my way,
Until the day fades into the gray.

The Heart's Unspoken Language

A heart that flutters like a bee on toast,
Whispers its secrets, it loves to boast.
Yet who understands this rambling song?
Is it right or just ridiculously wrong?

Pickles and ice cream, my favorite blend,
Tell me, dear friend, where does it end?
The whispers of desires, silly and sweet,
Like matching socks, a comical feat.

In the garden of giggles, we plant our dreams,
Watered with laughter, bursting at the seams.
A smile is a wink, a grin with a twist,
In the chaos of life, it's hard to resist.

So let's toast to misfits, every odd pair,
For in love's language, there's magic to share.
A dance with confusion, so easy to find,
In the sweet little secrets our hearts are entwined.

Serenade of the Unreliable

The clock says silly things, tick-tock, tick-tock,
I ponder the meaning while wearing my sock.
Fish in a hat tell me jokes on the line,
Unravel the threads, this riddle's divine!

Unreliable data from the cat on my lap,
Says "feed me my dreams" in a fur-coated nap.
Chaos reigns king while I sip on some tea,
What does it matter? I'm happy, you see!

Mustard and mayonnaise swirl in a dance,
While pondering why we wear socks in France.
The universe chuckles, and who can resist?
In the comedy of life, it's all but a twist.

So grab your umbrellas, we're off on a spree,
To follow the nonsense, wherever it be.
Laughs make the distance feel less like a mile,
In this grand adventure, let's linger a while.

Tides of the Unfathomable

Waves crash upon shores of whimsy and cheer,
Each bubble a question, each splash draws us near.
When the moon spills its milk on the ocean blue,
Do fish hold conferences on what we should do?

The sand whispers secrets caught in a breeze,
While flip-flops argue "Should we run or tease?"
Every grain of sand knows too much, they claim,
Yet all they can do is play silly games.

A dolphin with dreams of being a chef,
Whips up a feast but eats it himself.
Navigating waters of laughter and fun,
In a world that spins but never quite runs.

So toss me the tide where the wild things drift,
In the rhythm of nonsense, we'll find our gift.
Sink or swim, it's all quite the show,
In the tides of the unfathomable, let's go with the flow.

The Treasure of Living Questions

In a world of queries, we stroll along,
With signs all pointing, yet something feels wrong.
The map is a riddle, the compass is stuck,
We laugh at the chaos, what a peculiar luck!

Where's the treasure, they ask with a grin,
I say it's the laughter that flourishes within.
Each question a gem, each pause a delight,
We'll dance through the dark, finding joy in the night.

With socks that don't match and hats made of cheese,
We wander the maze, no plan as we please.
The answer eludes like a butterfly's flight,
But who needs directions when we feel so bright?

So gather the smiles, let's toast to the fun,
For living's the treasure, and we've already won!
In the quest full of questions, we find our own way,
With laughter as our guide, we'll brighten the day.

The Symphony of Ambiguous Days.

In a symphony played with mismatched notes,
We dance to the rhythm that tickles our throats.
The days are a jigsaw, scattered and wild,
Each moment a giggle, the universe smiled.

The clock spins backwards, or does it stand still?
With ice cream for breakfast, oh what a thrill!
In a world of confusion, we waltz and we sway,
Living's the melody, come join in the play.

The sun wears a tutu, the moon skates with flair,
While shadows are gossiping, light as aair.
With socks made of candy, we prance through the mist,
What's real and what's not? Ah, who can resist!

As trumpets keep blaring, off-key and fun,
We join in the chorus, hilariously spun.
Each question a note in our whimsical tale,
In the symphony's chaos, we'll never go pale.

Echoes of Uncertainty

In the hallways of doubt where echoes reside,
We giggle at whispers that tickle our pride.
What's true and what's not? Well, who really cares?
We'll spin in the haze with confetti in air!

The mirrors reflect what we want them to show,
Like a circus of mirrors, it's part of the show.
With laughter as our banner, we march through the fog,
Each chuckle a spark in this whimsical bog.

We juggle our worries, like oranges, bright,
Toss them in the air, let's mix day with night!
The riddle's the game, the joy is the quest,
In the echoes of chaos, we find we're the best.

So let's toast to the blunders, the slips and the falls,
In the symphony of life, we'll dance through the calls.
With joy as our anchor and laughs as our steer,
We'll surf through uncertainty, let's give a cheer!

The Dance of Shadows

In shadows we twirl, with laughter so spry,
As the moonlight giggles, and stars wink their eye.
We trip on the echoes of giggles and sighs,
With shoes made of dreams, we'll dance through the lies.

The shadows are partners in this absurd play,
They lead us in circles, then vanish away.
With every misstep, there's joyous delight,
We leap through the murk, our spirits take flight.

Like puppets on strings, we jiggle and sway,
With a wink and a nudge, we chase gloom away.
In the dance of the shadows, we wiggle and laugh,
Life's quirky conundrum, our own autograph!

So let's spin in the twilight, with woes left behind,
In the echoes of shadows, true joy we will find.
With hearts wide open, we'll prance and we'll preen,
In this dance of confusion, we'll conquer the scene!

www.ingramcontent.com/pod-product-compliance
Lightning Source LLC
Chambersburg PA
CBHW071834160426
43209CB00003B/287